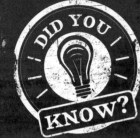

DID YOU KNOW?

SATURN COULD SAIL

and other fun facts

For Alexandra
—L. D.

For Ciara and Lauren
—H. E.

For Allison
—P. O.

To my wife, Lydia, and my daughter, Jackie Raye.
Thanks so much for all your love and support.
—A. S.

 LITTLE SIMON
An imprint of Simon & Schuster Children's Publishing Division
1230 Avenue of the Americas, New York, New York 10020
This Little Simon edition December 2014
Series concept by Laura Lyn DiSiena
Copyright © 2014 by Simon & Schuster, Inc.
All rights reserved, including the right of reproduction in whole or in part in any form.
LITTLE SIMON is a registered trademark of Simon & Schuster, Inc., and associated colophon is a trademark of Simon & Schuster, Inc.
For information about special discounts for bulk purchases, please contact Simon & Schuster Special Sales at 1-866-506-1949 or business@simonandschuster.com.
The Simon & Schuster Speakers Bureau can bring authors to your live event. For more information or to book an event contact the Simon & Schuster Speakers Bureau at 1-866-248-3049 or visit our website at
www.simonspeakers.com.
Designed by Ciara Gay
Manufactured in China 0914 SCP
10 9 8 7 6 5 4 3 2 1
Library of Congress Cataloging-in-Publication Data DiSiena, Laura Lyn, author. Saturn could sail : and other fun facts / by Laura Lyn DiSiena and Hannah Eliot. — First edition.pages cm. — (Did you know?)
Summary: "A book of fun facts about planets, stars, space ships, and more!"— Provided by publisher. Audience: Ages 4-8. Audience: K to grade 3.Includes bibliographical references and index.
1. Planets—Miscellanea—Juvenile literature. 2. Children's questions and answers. 3. Solar system—Miscellanea—Juvenile literature. 4. Outer space—Juvenile literature. I. Eliot, Hannah, author. II. Title.
QB602.D585 2015 523—dc23 2013050728
ISBN 978-1-4814-1429-6 (hc)
ISBN 978-1-4814-1428-9 (pbk)
ISBN 978-1-4814-1430-2 (eBook)

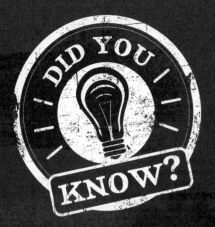
DID YOU KNOW?

SATURN COULD SAIL
and other fun facts

By Laura Lyn DiSiena and Hannah Eliot
Illustrated by Pete Oswald and Aaron Spurgeon

LITTLE SIMON
New York London Toronto Sydney New Delhi

3...2...1... BLAST OFF!

We're on our way to outer space. Come along for the ride!

Did you know that there are 8 planets in the solar system? Mercury, Venus, Earth, Mars, Jupiter, Saturn, Uranus, and Neptune. There used to be 9, but in 2006, Pluto was named a dwarf planet! Did you know that many of the planets have rings, but the rings on Saturn are the only ones that can be seen from Earth? How about that those rings are not solid? They're made up of bits of ice, rock, and dust! Or that Saturn spins so fast that 1 whole day is less than 11 hours. Okay, okay, maybe you knew those things . . .

But did you know that Saturn could SAIL?
You see, Saturn is the least dense planet in the solar system. It's made up mostly of gas.
(Earth, on the other hand, is made up of rocks and other matter.)
Because Saturn is so light, if there was a body of water big enough to hold it, it could float!
And if you stuck a mast on it, and added some cloth, it could sail, too!

You know what would *really* make Saturn sail? Some wind!
And do you know what planet has the fastest winds?
It's Neptune, the planet furthest from the sun. On Neptune, winds can
reach up to 1,500 miles per hour! Neptune is the fourth largest planet in
our solar system and is called an "ice giant" because it is made mostly of . . .

Did you know that every planet has seasons—just as Earth does? The length and type of the season depends on how tilted toward the sun each planet is. Let's go back to Neptune for a moment. Unlike the seasons on Earth, which each last 3 months, each season on Neptune lasts more than 40 years! The other planets have surprising season lengths as well. On Venus, seasons are pretty short—just about 2 months each. On Saturn, a season can last for 7 years, and on Jupiter, about 3 years!

SOLAR SYSTEM

The planets aren't only tilted *toward* the sun. They also revolve, or orbit, *around* the sun.
In fact, EVERYTHING in the solar system revolves around the sun. Do you know why?
It's because the gravitational pull of the sun is so powerful that it attracts all the other
objects to it. That's what gravity is—the force that attracts one object to another. It's also
the reason you're sitting or standing here right now! Earth's gravity is pulling you toward it.

And that this "spot" is actually a gigantic storm that has been raging on for hundreds of years? Jupiter is the largest planet in our solar system. It's so big that 1,300 Earths could fit in it!

Astronomers—scientists who study outer space—have been using telescopes to observe our solar system since the 1600s. But did you know that there wasn't an actual scientific definition for what a planet is until recently? The word "planet" comes from the Greek word "planetes," which means "wanderer." Unlike the stars astronomers were seeing, which were points of light fixed in one spot, some objects seemed to wander around the sky throughout the year. So they were called planets.

Do you know what the planets are really doing when they wander?
They are orbiting around the sun!

Astronomers may study the sky and space, but astronauts go *into* space!

The first person to go into space did so on April 12, 1961. Since then, only about 530 people have traveled there. Did you know that a space shuttle could travel so fast around the Earth that the people on board could see a sunrise or sunset every 45 minutes?!
Did you know that spacesuits protect astronauts from the extremely hot and cold temperatures of outer space?
Or that some astronauts train for spacewalks on what's called a Precision Air Bearing Floor? This is like a giant air-hockey table where jets of air allow the astronauts to move without friction. COOL!

Speaking of sports, during one space mission, an astronaut named Alan Shepard hit a golf ball while on the moon! Actually, he hit 2 golf balls . . . and they're both still there. Do you know what else is probably still on the moon? The footprints of anyone who has ever visited it. And why is that? It's because there is no atmosphere on the moon, so there's no wind or water to destroy the footprints!

Have you ever seen a bright streak of light across the night sky? Do you know what that's called? A shooting star! AMAZING! But did you know that a shooting star isn't a star at all? It's actually a small piece of rock or dust called a meteoroid that moves really fast—sometimes as much as 160,000 miles per hour. When it passes through Earth's atmosphere, it burns up, leaving a bright tail behind it.

Does this have you wondering what a regular star is made of?

Well, a star is a huge sphere of very hot, glowing gas.
TWINKLE! TWINKLE! Stars come in a variety of
sizes and colors. Can you believe that our sun, as big as it is,
is just an average-sized star? Averaged-sized stars are yellow,
while small stars are reddish, and large ones are blue.
Astronomers have even discovered a star composed entirely of diamond!

A constellation is a very distinct and recognizable pattern of stars in the sky.
You can see these patterns by connecting the stars, just as you would connect the dots!
Some of the patterns make animals or objects that are familiar to us.
Something you might not know is that the sun is the only star in *our* solar system.
All the stars that we see at night when we are looking at the constellations are
actually in solar systems far away. WOW!

Have you ever wondered why the moon looks yellow or orange—especially when it first rises at night? This is due to the atmosphere. You see, when the moon is near the horizon, there's a lot of atmosphere for its light to pass through. By the time the moonlight gets to your eyes, the green, blue, and purple parts of the visible light have been scattered by air molecules, so you see only yellow, orange, or red!

It takes the moon about 27 days to orbit around Earth, and during that time, the moon goes through 8 phases.

The moon is known for having tons of craters on it. And where did those craters come from, you ask? They came from comets and asteroids that crashed into the moon billions of years ago!

Comets are cosmic snowballs made up of frozen gases, dust, and rock. Comets come from the Kuiper Belt and the Oort Cloud. These "snowballs" may have crashed into Earth as well, and that's where Earth may have gotten its water!

Asteroids, on the other hand, are metallic, rocky bodies. They can be found in an asteroid belt with thousands of other asteroids orbiting the sun.

Did you know there
is something in space that we
cannot see no matter how powerful
a telescope we look through? It's called a
BLACK HOLE. That's a place in space where
gravity's pull is so strong that not even one
bit of light can get out! Even though they are
technically invisible, special telescopes that float
in space can help find black holes. They spot
them because stars that are near the
holes give off high-energy light.

Astronomers think that there may be millions of black holes in Earth's galaxy. By the way, do you know what Earth's galaxy is called? It's the Milky Way! And the reason we say "Earth's galaxy" is because there are actually hundreds of billions of galaxies in the universe.

The Milky Way is a very active galaxy. It's constantly changing. In fact, did you know that new stars are born all the time in our galaxy? A team of astronomers is still trying to figure out exactly how many stars are produced and how often, but they think it's about 7 new stars per year.

Stars are born in large, cold clouds of gas and dust. These are called "nebulas."
The clouds eventually start to shrink under their own gravity, and as they get smaller, they
break apart into pieces. Then the temperature of these pieces starts to rise. When it hits about
20 million degrees Fahrenheit—whew! That's hot!—the pieces become stars!

The farthest a spacecraft has ever gone is to the edge of our solar system.
Voyager 1, a research craft launched into space in 1977 flew past Jupiter and Saturn. It even discovered active volcanoes on one of Jupiter's moons! *Voyager 1* continues to float in space. It carries with it a greeting message of sounds and images that show life and culture on Earth in case it ever meets any form of life!

Did you know that in the same year *Voyager 1* was launched, so was *Voyager 2*? *Voyager 2*'s purpose was to explore Uranus and Neptune, which it has done! And since Uranus is made mostly of ice, and Neptune is made of a solid core surrounded by gas, unlike Saturn, those planets sure couldn't SAIL!

MORE FUN FACTS

Saturn: Saturn contains helium—the same kind of gas you pump into balloons!

Astronomy: You can be an astronomer too! Just go to a planetarium, a building with a domelike structure where you can see projections of the solar system!

Star: A star's brightness depends on its luminosity, meaning how much energy it puts out.

Gravity: Sir Isaac Newton, one of the scientists who helped develop the laws of universal gravitation and motion, may have first started thinking about gravity when he saw an apple fall from a tree!

Astronauts: Astronauts grow in space! Without gravity, the spine expands, making them taller.

Comets: Halley's Comet last appeared in the inner solar system in 1986. It will return again sometime in 2061, so get your cameras ready!.

Neptune: In Neptune's atmosphere, there is a large white cloud that "scoots" around, so we call it "Scooter!"

Nebula: The Orion Nebula is visible to the naked eye.

Constellation: The brightest star in the night sky is not the North Star. It's Sirius, and it can be found in the Canis Major constellation.

Uranus: The axis of Uranus is sideways in comparison to other planets, meaning that its north and south poles are in line with the equators of other planets!

Space shuttle: Space shuttles had laboratories in them, which allowed scientists to perform experiments in microgravity.

Mercury: Like Venus, Mercury has no moons.

Moon: The Earth's tides are mostly caused by the gravitational pull of the moon.

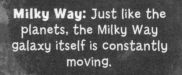

Milky Way: Just like the planets, the Milky Way galaxy itself is constantly moving.